a Mighty Wind

A Mighty Wind

by

C. I. SCOFIELD

BAKER BOOK HOUSE

GRAND RAPIDS, MICHIGAN

Reprinted 1973
by Baker Book House Company
ISBN: 0-8010-7982-9
Printed in the United States of America

Third printing, May 1976

Contents

Introduction

Introduction

We are in the midst of a marked revival of interest in the Person and work of the Holy Spirit. More books, booklets and tracts upon that subject have issued from the press during the last eighty years than in all previous time since the invention of printing. Indeed, within the last twenty years more has been written and said upon the doctrine of the Holy Spirit than in the preceding eighteen hundred years. Doubtless much good has been done. Doubtless in so far as the testimony has been according to the Scripture it has been the divine answer alike to the false mysticism of the day—spiritualism, theosophy, Christian science (falsely so called)—and to the current denial of the supernatural which is enervating modern Christianity.

But along with this good is much evil. Much which has been written and said is distinctly unbiblical; much, of which so strong a statement would not be warranted, has the grave demerit of interpreting Scripture by experience, instead of subjecting experience to the test of Scripture. Something is confidently asserted because the writer has "felt" it. Not infrequently the Spirit has been put into the place of Christ. Much of this mass of testimony is deeply legal in its spirit. Believers are set upon various works to the end that they may receive the baptism with the Spirit. They are directed to pray, to empty themselves, to cleanse themselves, to die to self and the world. Husbands and wives are directed to "die" to each other. Natural affection is branded as idolatry. In many ways asceticism is inculcated, and made conditional if the Spirit is to be received in His fullness.

Very few of the more recent writings upon the Holy Spirit distinguish the dispensational aspects of the question, or take account of the progressive unfolding of the doctrine of His Person and work. In these papers the endeavor will be made to state these vital things with clearness and simplicity. At present it may suffice to say, that in respect of no other doctrine of Scripture is an understanding of its progressive revelation more absolutely essential. The writings referred to add to the confusion of mingling together the past, middle-past, and present offices and operations of the Spirit, the farther discord of presenting the personal experiences of the Apostles as the pattern of the believer's experience now. The fact that the Apostles began as Jews after the flesh, went on to be spiritual Jews, the true Israel of God, seeing in Jesus the promised Messiah, and then to be, with Christ as chief corner-stone, the foundation stones of the church, seems utterly forgotten by the more part of recent writers upon the Holy Spirit. They speak of new Pentecosts without reflecting that they might with equal appropriateness speak of new Nativities. It should be obvious to the most careless student of Scripture that just as the Son of God had been acting in and toward the world from the first, but at last made a true Advent at the Nativity; so the Holy Spirit, who had been acting in and toward the world from the first, at last made a true Advent at Pentecost. Furthermore, it is rare indeed to find the *relationships* of the Spirit properly associated with His *offices*. In Scripture these are carefully discriminated. The undeniable result of all this is that many earnest children of God are in utter confusion of mind upon this profoundly vital subject; and the peril is that in very weariness and discouragement thousands will turn from the study of the doctrine of the Holy Spirit, as thousands have turned from the study of types and prophecies, sadly convinced that the truth is so hidden away as that no one may hope to come to clearness of vision of it.

The present writer is persuaded, on the contrary, that, while many of the *operations* of the Spirit (as His agency in the new birth) are beyond human analysis and definition, the doctrine of His person, relationships, and offices is transparently simple. The purpose, then, of these Plain Papers is to set forth that doctrine in a plain and Biblical way. That is all. The reader of these Papers will not, therefore, expect them to constitute an elaborate treatise; still less to present or defend a theory. The writer aspires to do no more than to set in order things which are in confusion, and to leave his readers face to face with their actual privileges and responsibilities in respect of the divine Spirit who came into the world on the day of Pentecost for purposes as definite and simple as those which, some thirty-three years before Pentecost, brought the divine Son into the world.

The Holy Spirit Is a Divine Person

I

The Holy Spirit Is a Divine Person

The complete demonstration of this fundamental fact would require the citation of every passage in the Scriptures relating in any way to the Holy Spirit, since every reference to Him implies or asserts both His personality and His Deity. It must, therefore, suffice to gather under convenient heads, examples of such passages. *First: The Holy Spirit is a Person, as distinguished from an influence, emanation, or manifestation.*

This appears from the following considerations: (1) The same words, implying personality, are used of Him in Scripture which are used of other persons.

The following may suffice as examples of this class of passages, and to these the reader may add largely. "And I will pray the Father, and he shall give you another Comforter, that he may abide with you forever. Even the Spirit of truth; whom the world cannot receive, because it seeth him not, neither knoweth him: but ye know him; for he dwelleth with you, and shall be in you. But the Comforter which is the Holy Ghost whom the Father will send in my name, he shall teach you all things, and bring all things to your remembrance, whatsoever I have said unto you" (John 14:16, 17, 26). "Nevertheless I tell you the truth; It is expedient for you that I go away: for if I go not away, the Comforter will not come unto you; but if I depart, I will send him unto you. And when he is come, he will reprove the world of sin, and of righteousness and of judgment. Howbeit when he, the Spirit of truth, is come, he will guide you into all truth: for he shall not speak of himself; but whatsoever he shall hear, *that* shall he speak: and he will show you things to come. He shall glorify me: for he shall receive of mine, and shall show *it* unto you. All things that the Father hath are mine: therefore said I, that he shall take of mine, and shall show *it* unto you" (John 16:7, 8, 13-15).

(2) Men are said to act toward Him in ways which would be impossible or absurd if He were not truly a Person.

Of this class of passages, also, a few examples must suffice. "But they rebelled, and vexed his Holy Spirit: therefore he was turned to be their enemy, *and* he fought against them" (Isaiah 63:10). "Wherefore I say unto you, All manner of sin and blasphemy shall be forgiven unto men: but the blasphemy *against* the Holy Ghost shall not be forgiven unto men" (Matthew 12:31). "And grieve not the Holy Spirit of God, whereby ye are sealed unto the day of redemption" (Ephesians 4:30). "Of how much sorer punishment, suppose ye, shall he be thought worthy, who hath trodden under foot the Son of God, and hath counted the blood of the covenant, wherewith he was sanctified, an unholy thing, and hath done despite unto the Spirit of Grace?" (Hebrews 10:29).

(3) The Holy Spirit is said to perform actions which would be possible only to a person.

The following passages sufficiently illustrate this: "That which is born of the flesh is flesh; and that which is born of the Spirit is spirit" (John 3:6). "But the Comforter which is the Holy Ghost, whom the Father will send in my name, he shall teach you all things, and bring all things to your remembrance whatsoever I have said unto you" (John 14:26; see also passages quoted above under sub-head [I].) "Then the Spirit said unto Philip, Go near, and join thyself to this chariot" (Acts 8:29). "While Peter thought on the vision, the Spirit said unto him Behold, three men seek thee" (Acts 10:19). "As they ministered to the Lord, and fasted, the Holy Ghost said, Separate me Barnabas and Saul" (Acts 13:2). "And in like manner the Spirit also helpeth our infirmity: for we know not how to pray as we ought; but the Spirit himself maketh intercession for us with groanings which cannot be uttered" (Romans 8:26, R.V.). "Now when they had gone throughout Phrygia and the region of Galatia, and were forbidden of the Holy Ghost to preach the word in Asia, after they were come to Mysia, they assayed to go into Bithynia: but the Spirit suffered them not" (Acts 16:6, 7).

Here the Spirit is represented as the active agent in the believer's re-birth; as teaching, reproving, guiding, speaking, receiving, shewing, as giving active and specific direction to the service of the saints, and as praying. It would be difficult to say how the idea of personality could be more elaborately presented.

Secondly: The Holy Spirit is a Divine Person; in the proper sense, Deity.

Let it be noted: (1) He is called God. "Also I heard the voice of the Lord, saying, Whom shall I send, and who will go for us? Then said I, Here *am* I, send me. And he said, Go and tell this people, Hear ye indeed, but understand not; and see ye indeed, but perceive not." "Well spake the Holy Ghost by Esaias the prophet unto our fathers, Saying, Go unto this people, and say, Hearing ye shall not hear, and shall not understand; and seeing ye shall see, and not perceive" (Isaiah 6:8, 9, with Acts 28:25, 26).

The bearing of these two passages is obvious. Isaiah says he heard the voice of the Lord, Luke that the Holy Ghost spake; the completed truth being that God the Holy Ghost spoke. (See, as another like instance, Jeremiah 31:31-34, with Hebrews 10:15.)

"But we all, with unveiled face reflecting like a mirror the glory of the Lord, are transformed into the same image from glory to glory, even as from the Lord the Spirit." (II Corinthians 3:18, R.V.). "But Peter said, Ananias, why hath Satan filled thine heart to lie to the Holy Ghost, and to keep back part of the price of the land? While it remained, was it not thine own? and after it was sold, was it not in thine own power? why hast thou conceived this thing in thine heart? thou hast not lied unto men, but unto God" (Acts 5:3, 4.)

The declaration is explicit: to lie to the Holy Ghost is to lie to God.

(2) The Scriptures constantly ascribe to the Holy Spirit the attributes of God, as omnipotence, omniscience, omnipresence, and also His highest perfection, holiness. Holiness, indeed, is the emphatic mark of the Spirit. And this not as having been made or become holy, but as being holy, and Himself the producer of holiness.

"Whither shall I go from thy Spirit? or whither shall I flee from thy presence? If I ascend up into heaven, thou *art* there: if I make my bed in hell, behold thou *art there*. *If* I take the wings of the morning, *and* dwell in the uttermost parts of the sea; even there shall thy hand lead me and thy right hand shall hold me" (Psalm 139:7-10, etc.). "And the earth was without form, and void; and darkness *was* upon the face of the deep. And the Spirit of God moved upon the face of the waters" (Genesis 1:2). "By his Spirit he hath garnished the heavens" (Job 26:13). "But as it is written, Eye hath not seen, nor ear heard, neither have entered into the heart of man the things which God hath prepared for them that love him. But God hath revealed *them* unto us by his Spirit: for the Spirit searcheth all things, yea, the deep things of God. For what man knoweth the things of a man, save the spirit of man which is in him? even so the things of God knoweth no man, but the Spirit of God" (I Corinthians 2:9-11). "How much more shall the blood of Christ, who through the eternal Spirit offered himself without spot to God, purge your conscience from dead works to serve the living God?" (Hebrews 9:14).

(3) He is represented as performing works possible only to Deity. This is shown by every one of the passages quoted in the

last preceding paragraph, to which may be added the following:

"The Spirit of God hath made me, and the breath of the Almighty hath given me life" (Job 33:4). "Thou sendest forth thy Spirit, they are created: and thou renewest the face of the earth" (Psalm 104:30). "But if the Spirit of him that raised up Jesus from the dead dwell in you, he that raised up Christ from the dead shall also quicken your mortal bodies by his Spirit that dwelleth in you" (Romans 8:11). "And such were some of you: but ye are washed, but ye are sanctified, but ye are justified in the name of the Lord Jesus, and by the Spirit of our God" (I Corinthians 6:11). "For the prophecy came not in old time by the will of man: but holy men of God spake *as they were* moved by the Holy Ghost" (II Peter 1:21). "Men *and* brethren, this scripture must needs have been fulfilled, which the Holy Ghost by the mouth of David spake before concerning Judas" (Acts 1:16). "And when they bring you unto the synagogues, and *unto* magistrates, and powers, take ye no thought how or what thing ye shall answer, or what ye shall say: for the Holy Ghost shall teach you in the same hour what ye ought to say" (Luke 12:11, 12). "Take heed therefore unto yourselves, and to all the flock, over the which the Holy Ghost hath made you overseers, to feed the church of God, which he hath purchased with his own blood" (Acts 20:28). "For to one is given by the Spirit the word of wisdom; to another the gifts of healing by the same Spirit; to another the working of miracles; to another prophecy; to another discerning of spirits; to another divers kinds of tongues; to another the interpretation of tongues; but all these worketh that one and the selfsame Spirit, dividing to every man severally as he will" (I Corinthians 12:8-11).

Surely it would be impossible intelligently to impute to a mere influence such definite personal acts as these; or to suppose one less than absolute Deity able to perform them.

In conclusion it is enough to say that further proofs both of the personality and Deity of the Spirit may be found in the facts that it is possible to sin against Him; that He is joined on terms of perfect equality with the Father and the Son in the baptismal formula; and that in seven remarkable passages in the second and third chapters of the Revelation, we are commanded to "hear what the Spirit saith unto the churches." There is no biblical reason for believing in the Deity and personality of the Father or of the Son, which does not equally establish that of the Spirit.

The Holy Spirit Before and Since Pentecost

2

The Holy Spirit Before and Since Pentecost

It is obvious to every reader of the Bible that the doctrine of the Holy Spirit follows, in common with every other doctrine, the law of progressive development. In Scripture nothing is completely told at once. "First the blade, then the ear; after that the full corn in the ear," is ever the divine method of revelation. If we seek for the natural divisions in this progressive unfolding of the truth concerning the Spirit, we shall find them so broadly marked off as to be unmistakable. These divisions are:

1. The Holy Spirit before the Incarnation of Christ.

2. The Holy Spirit in relation to the Person and ministry of Christ from the Incarnation to Pentecost.

3. The Holy Spirit from Pentecost to the opening of the door to the Gentiles.

4. The Holy Spirit in His present offices and relationships as defined in the Epistles.

5. The Holy Spirit (prophetically) in the future kingdom age.

The purpose of this Paper is briefly to sketch the development of the doctrine in the first four aspects of its fivefold order, and to note the distinctions which may save us from confusion of thought.

First: The Holy Spirit before the Incarnation

In the Old Testament the Holy Spirit is revealed, as we have seen in the preceding Paper, as a divine Person. As such He is associated in the work of creation (Genesis 1:2; Job 26:13; 27:3; 33:4; Psalm 104:30; etc.); strives with sinful man (Genesis 6:3); enlightens the Spirit of man (Job 32:8; Proverbs 20:27); gives skill of hand (Exodus 31:2-5); bestows physical strength (Judges 14:6); and qualifies the servants of God for a various ministry (Exodus 33:3; 35:21-31; Numbers 11:25-29; Judges 11:29; etc.; I Samuel 16:17; II Samuel 23:2). To this should be added that operation of the Spirit by which the men of faith in the Old Testament ages were regenerated. While this doctrine is not explicitly taught in the Old Testament (except prophetically), our Lord's words in John 3:5 and Luke 13:28 leave no doubt as to the fact itself. Since the new birth is essential to seeing and entering the kingdom of God, and since the Old Testament saints are in that kingdom, it follows necessarily that they were born of the Spirit. But, since that was the period of nonage, as Paul explains (Galatians 3—4), they had not the indwelling Spirit of sonship. They were minors, "under tutors and governors."

It should be remembered, also, that to the Old Testament saint no way was revealed by which he might receive the Holy Spirit. All the offices of the Spirit were reserved within the sovereign will of God. He sent His Spirit upon whosoever He would. That the Spirit came upon an individual did not by any means prove him to be in salvation. Even a sincere believer had no assurance that the Spirit might not forsake him (Psalm 51:11); whereas the believer of this dispensation has as express promise of the abiding of the Spirit.

Secondly: The Holy Spirit in relation to the Person and ministry of Christ from His conception to Pentecost.

The Four Gospels present the Spirit in connection with the person and ministry of

Christ. Our Lord is conceived by the Holy Spirit, filled with the Holy Spirit, baptized, and led by Him. In His power Christ casts out demons, and performs His astonishing works (Luke 1:15, 35; 3:21, 22; 4:1, 18; Matthew 12:28). He is pointed out by John as the Baptizer with the Holy Ghost, and this testimony Christ confirms in His last discourse (Matthew 3:11; Acts 1:4, 5).

Furthermore, our Lord taught His personal disciples how they, too, might have the Spirit. "If ye then, being evil, know how to give good gifts unto your children; how much more shall your heavenly Father give the Holy Spirit to them that ask him?" (Luke 11:13).

So familiar are we with this passage that we little think with what astonishment our Lord's words must have fallen upon the ears of His disciples. Doubtless they were acquainted with the prophecy of Joel, but that pointed to a sovereign act of God wholly without reference to prayer or any other human condition. Up to that time, as we have seen, no means had been made known by the use of which any and every man of faith might obtain the Spirit. In Old Testament times the Spirit came upon some men as God's service required, but these cases were rare, occasional and exceptional. All was purely within the sovereign will of God. But now to the whole body of disciples came the astonishing statement that any one of them, simply by asking, might receive the Spirit! The privilege was too great for their faith. Not only is there not the smallest evidence that any of those disciples asked and obtained the gift of the Spirit, but there is the most conclusive evidence that none of them did so ask and obtain.

At the close of His earth-ministry our Lord defined the *person, relationships* and *offices* of the coming Spirit.

(1) Since they had not prayed the Father for the Spirit, *He* would. "I will pray the Father, and he shall give you another Comforter, that he may abide with you forever" (John 14:16). "But when the Comforter is come, whom I will send unto you from the Father," etc. "If I depart I will send him unto you" (John 15:26; 16:7).

(2) The coming One should stand related to believers in a threefold way. "He dwelleth *with* you, and shall be *in* you" (John 14:17). "Behold I send the promise of my Father *upon* you" (John 14:17; Luke 24:49). The coming One should be "with" men, convicting, converting, regenerating; "within" men, as a fountain of living water, cleansing, renewing, satisfying; "upon" men, bestowing gifts and power for service. He should be Comforter, Guide, Teacher, Revealer.

(3) Himself leaving the body of revealed

truth incomplete, Christ promised that the Spirit of truth should complete it (John 16:13). Then He went to the cross.

Beginning, on the very day of His resurrection, His new ministry, He fulfilled, for His disciples, the promise, "He shall be *in* you" (John 14:17; 20:22). On the evening of His resurrection, our Lord "breathed on them, and saith unto them, Receive ye the Holy Ghost." They had not, then, already received Him. Nor, let it be observed, did they then receive Him by claiming the promise, "much more shall your heavenly Father give the Holy Spirit to them that ask him" (Luke 11:13). Christ, shewing His hands and His side, the proof that redemption was fully accomplished, as "first-fruits" (Romans 8:23) and "seal" (Ephesians 1:13) of that redemption, imparted the indwelling Spirit to the men who believed on Him. It was their privilege, as believers, now that the blood of atonement had been shed, *without other condi-tion*, to receive the Spirit. He was the "earnest of their inheritance" (Ephesians 1:14). Absolutely the only condition *in them* was faith on the Lord Jesus Christ. That impartation of the Spirit as indwelling the believer simply and only because he was a believer, marked the tremendous transition from the age of law to the age of Grace.

But there was yet another relationship of the Spirit, the baptism, or the "upon" rela tionship, for which these disciples who had received the Spirit as indwelling, were com-manded to wait. "Behold I send the pro-mise of my Father upon you: but tarry ye in the city of Jerusalem, until ye be endued with power from on high" (Luke 24:49). "For John truly baptized with water; but ye shall be baptized with the Holy Ghost, not many days hence. But ye shall receive power, after that the Holy Ghost is come upon you: and ye shall be witnesses unto me, both in Jerusalem, and in all Judæa, and in Samaria, and unto the uttermost part of the earth" (Acts 1:5, 8).

Then He was parted from them; and the "tarrying" began.

The Holy Spirit Before and Since Pentecost

(CONTINUED)

3

The Holy Spirit Before and Since Pentecost

Two of the divisions into which the progressive unfolding of the doctrine of the Holy Spirit falls have been reviewed: the Old Testament stage of that doctrine, and the period covered by the presence of Christ on earth. We now reach:

Thirdly: The Holy Spirit from Pentecost to the Opening of the Kingdom to the Gentiles.

Until the day of Pentecost, the disciples, who had received, by the outbreathing of

Christ, the *indwelling* Spirit, waited for His coming "upon" them; and when that day was fully come, with the outward manifestations of sound and flame, He came. They were baptized with the Holy Ghost; and not only baptized, but "*filled* with the Holy Ghost." Three results of that baptism and filling were at once manifest: (1) *gift*—"they began to speak with other tongues as the Spirit gave them utterance"; (2) *power*—as Peter preached the hearers were "pricked in their heart," and "there were added unto them about three thousand souls"; and (3) *unity*—"and all that believed were together, and had all things common."

This outward unity was the result, not alone of the fact that they were alike believers in one Lord, and committed to one common destiny, but was the manifestation of a new fact concerning them which had been accomplished for them by the baptism with the Spirit; they had been, by that baptism, *vitally* united to each other, and to the risen Christ. Then began to be formed that "body" of Christ, of which the Lord Jesus, at the right hand of the Father is the Head, and all regenerate believers at and since Pentecost, are the members. "For as the body is one, and hath many members, and all the members of that one body, being many, are one body; so also is Christ. For by one Spirit are we all baptized into one body, whether we be Jews or Gentiles, whether we be bond or free" (I Corinthians 12:12, 13). (See, also, Ephesians 1:20-23; 4:3-16.)

This was that vital union with the risen and glorified Christ of which our Lord had spoken (John 15:1-10), as the union of the vine and the branches. The unity, then, which at and after Pentecost, was manifested outwardly by their being "together," and having "all things common," was wrought by the baptism with the Holy Spirit. *Gift*, or special enduement for distinctive service; *power*, or the ministry of that gift in Divine energy; and *union* to the body of Christ, are the results of the baptism and filling with the Holy Spirit.

From the day of Pentecost, when Peter used the first key and opened the kingdom to the Jews, to the memorable day when, in the house of Cornelius, he used the second key and opened the door to the Gentiles, the impartation of the Spirit to believers (all Jewish) was marked by two peculiarities which disappear entirely in the case of Gentile converts. These were (1) that commonly an interval of time elapsed between the receiving of Christ by faith, and the baptism with the Spirit. And (2) that commonly the mediation of the disciples, either by prayer or by the laying on of hands, was necessary. Instances may be found by reference to Acts 8:12-17; 9:17.

The whole of this period (Acts 2—9, inclusive) is peculiar, transitional and Jewish.

Fourth: The Holy Spirit since the opening of the door to the Gentiles, in His present relationships and offices as defined in the Epistles.

With the opening of the kingdom to the Gentiles (Acts 10) we reach what may be called the normal experience for this dispensation. It is very simply stated by Luke in Acts 10:44: "*While Peter yet spake these words*, the Holy Ghost fell on all them which heard the word." Peter's own account of it is in Acts 11:15: "And as I began to speak, the Holy Ghost fell on them, as on us at the beginning."

Henceforth, wherever the gospel is believed among Gentiles, the Holy Spirit in the moment when they believe, regenerates and indwells them, and baptizes them into the Body of Christ. To this the Epistles bear constant and unvarying testimony. A few examples of the Epistolary testimony must suffice.

As to His indwelling: "What! know ye not that your body is the temple of the Holy Ghost which is in you, which ye have of God?" (I Corinthians 6:19).

It should be remembered that this is said of the most carnal and unsanctified body of believers mentioned in the New Testament. For their low, unspiritual state see I Corinthians 1:11, 12; 3:1-4; 5:1; 6:1. Indeed, the Apostle makes this great truth of the indwelling of the Spirit a basis for exhorting them to abstain from the coarsest sins. They had not attained to the indwelling by acts of obedience, nor by peculiar saintliness. The indwelling was the result of their position as Gentiles saved by grace.

"Now if any man have not the Spirit of Christ, he is none of his" (Romans 8:9).

"For ye have not received the spirit of

bondage again to fear; but ye have received the Spirit of adoption, whereby we cry, Abba, Father" (Romans 8:15).

"And because ye are sons, God hath sent forth the Spirit of his Son into your hearts, crying, Abba, Father" (Galatians 4:6).

Briefly, as to the fact of the baptism, note:

"For, as the body is one, and hath many members, and all the members of that one body, being many, are one body; so also is Christ. For in one Spirit *were we all baptized* into one body, and were all made to drink of one Spirit" (I Corinthians 12:12, 13, R.V.). This also was written to the same "carnal" Corinthians, who, so far from having made great progress in the divine life, thus "attaining" the "second blessing," were "babes in Christ," living upon milk, and not meat.

Note, farther, in that twelfth chapter, the emphasis upon the universality of this position "in Christ" among believers: "*Every* man," verse 11; "*all* the members," verse 12; "*all* baptized," verse 13; "*all* made to drink," verse 13; "*every one*," verse 18; "*ye* are the body of Christ," verse 27.

In other words, the body of Christ is formed of individual believers united to Christ, the living Head, by the baptism with the Holy Spirit; and, in this sense, there are no *disjecta membra*, no "unattached" members of Christ. The idea is wholly absent from the Epistles, and would never have entered the mind of man from the reading of the Epistles. The blinding, misleading notion that a Gentile may be a regenerate believer in the Lord Jesus Christ, and yet be destitute of the indwelling and baptizing Spirit, is wholly due to the failure to observe the progress of doctrine in the New Testament concerning the Spirit.

Doubtless, also, the strange notion that

the experiences through which the personal disciples of our Lord passed from their position as mere Jews in the flesh, to their ultimate place in the body of Christ, must be followed by all subsequent believers, whether Jew or Gentile, is all part responsible for the error. The startling experience of the household of Cornelius should have sufficed to dispel it. That experience shook the apostolic church to its foundation, and was the determining factor in the decision of the Jerusalem council (Acts 15:7-10), which, under God, emancipated the Gospel from its Jewish fetters.

Instead of teaching believers today that they are destitute of the Spirit unless they have passed through some experience subsequent to conversion; or that they may obtain the Spirit by asking the Father, as in the interregnum between the baptism and crucifixion of Christ; or that many must be with one accord in one place, "on their faces before God" if they would receive the Spirit; or that they cannot receive the Spirit until they are "entirely consecrated," or "fully yielded"; they should be solemnly charged with the responsibility which rests upon them as those whose bodies are already "temples of the Holy Ghost"; as those who *are* "members in particular" of the sacred body of Christ. They should be exhorted: "Grieve not the Holy Spirit of God, *whereby ye are sealed* unto the day of redemption" (Ephesians 4:30); and they should be shown the glorious possibilities of blessing latent in those facts.

No more transforming thought can be received into a believer's mind than that his body is already indwelt by the Holy Spirit, and that he is now a member of the body of Christ.

The misleading opinion that it is possible to be a true believer and yet to remain for a time destitute of the Spirit is sometimes justified by the case of the "disciples" whom Paul found at Ephesus, of whom he asked—not, as in the Authorized Version, "Have ye received the Holy Ghost since ye believed?"—but, as in the Revised Version, "Received ye the Holy Spirit when ye believed?" (Acts 19:2). As to this case it is sufficient to say:

(1) The very form of the apostle's question indicates that, normally, they should have received the Holy Spirit when they believed (literally, "upon believing").

(2) The question developed the true state of the case, they were not Christ's disciples at all, but John the Baptist's. This marks them as Jews or Jewish proselytes. They were in the precise state of John's disciples before he pointed to Jesus, "the Lamb of God that taketh away the sins of the world," as the alone object of faith.

(3) That they had not the Spirit was due, not to their ignorance of His advent at

Pentecost, but to the fact that their faith was not in Christ crucified, but only the proper Jewish expectation of a coming Messiah (verse 4).

(4) That they were not Christians previously to this interview with Paul, is proved by the fact he added Christian baptism to the mere preparatory rite of John the Baptist (verse 5).

But, while it is true that every regenerate believer is indwelt by the Spirit, and by the Spirit baptized into Christ, it is of the very deepest moment to note that the Acts and Epistles discriminate between *possessing* the Spirit, and being *filled* with the Spirit. An example of this discrimination may be seen in Ephesians. In Ephesians 4:30 the believer is reminded (as previously in 1:13) that he *is* sealed with the Spirit; in verse 18, he is commanded to be "*filled* with the Spirit." Doubtless, many believers are filled with the Spirit when (in the moment of conversion) He regenerates, indwells and baptizes them. The disciples at Pentecost were both baptized and filled with the Spirit (Acts 2:1-4). After describing the physical manifestations attending their baptism, the account adds: "and they were all filled with the Holy Ghost."

That all believers are not "filled with the Spirit" when He takes up His abode in them, and baptizes them into Christ, is due to the fact that they have complied with the condition for the receiving of the Spirit, which is simply faith in Christ (John 7:39; Galatians 3:2), but have not complied with the conditions for the filling with the Spirit. These will be set forth in the following chapter.

It should be added here that, while the filling with the Spirit is as definite an act of divine power as the baptism with the Spirit, the filling, unlike the baptism, may be many time repeated. The true formula is:

"one baptism; many fillings" (W. J. Erdman). The sealing is "unto the day of redemption," and therefore needs not to be repeated (Ephesians 1:13, 14; 4:30). "The anointing which ye have received of him abideth" (I John 2:27).

An illustration, both of the distinction between the baptism and the filling, and of the difference between possessing the Spirit and being filled with the Spirit, is found in the comparison of Acts 2:1-4 and Acts 4:23-31. Here the same disciples who were both baptized and filled with the Spirit on the day of Pentecost, were again filled with the Spirit. Had they lost their seal? Surely not, for they were "sealed unto the day of redemption" (Ephesians 4:30). Had they become unbaptized out of the body of Christ? Surely not. They had become afraid of the Sanhedrin—"Lord, behold their threatenings"—and thus were quenching the Spirit, and the remedy was re-filling.

"The place was shaken where they were assembled together; and they were all filled with the Holy Ghost, and they spake the word of God with boldness."

It should be added that in the Acts and Epistles it is not the facts of the indwelling and baptism with the Spirit which are accounted as bestowing blessing in life, and power in service, but the state of being filled with the Spirit. Not men *having* the Spirit are sought for service, but men *filled* with the Holy Ghost.

The
Filling with
the Holy Spirit

4

The Filling with the Holy Spirit

In the last chapter the writer endeavored to show that the Epistles, which (with the Revelation) are God's final word to the saints of this dispensation, instead of exhorting believers to seek the indwelling of the Spirit, or the baptism with the Spirit, again and again assert that both the indwelling and the baptism are the present possession of all who, through faith in the Lord Jesus Christ, are regenerate; and that exhortations to holiness of life are based upon the already existing fact of such possession. It was shown, further, that not the presence merely of the Spirit as indwelling and baptizing secured the fullness of blessing, victory, and power, but the state of being filled with the Spirit. Ephesians 5:18 is a distinct command to "be filled with the Spirit." The purpose of the present paper is to point out the simple Biblical conditions of such filling. These conditions are (1) *negative*—some things must *not* be, if we are to know this blessing; and (2) *positive* —demanding a definite affirmative action upon our part.

1. *The negative conditions of the filling with the Holy Spirit.*

(1) The first of these negative conditions is stated in Ephesians 4:30, 31. "And grieve not the Holy Spirit of God, whereby ye are sealed unto the day of redemption." The word rendered "grieve" in this passage means literally "to make sorrowful." It is a

touching thought that the Bible never speaks of the wrath of the Spirit. The one passage in the Authorized Version (Isaiah 63:10) in which the Spirit is said to be "vexed," is a mistranslation which the Revised Version correctly changes to "grieved." It is not strange that some have found in this susceptibility of the Spirit to be grieved but not angered the mother part of the divine love.

The things which grieve the Spirit are unholy things allowed in the life. Some of these are enumerated in verse 31, immediately following the exhortation not to grieve the Spirit: "Bitterness, and wrath, and anger, and clamor, and evil speaking, with all malice." In Galatians 5:17 we are told that "the flesh lusteth against the Spirit, and the Spirit against the flesh"; and the "works of the flesh" are enumerated: "Adultery, fornication, uncleanness, lasciviousness, idolatry, witchcraft, hatred, variance, emulations, wrath, strife, seditions, heresies, envyings, murders, drunkenness, revelings, *and such like*"; a clause which covers every manifestation of the flesh. All these grieve the Spirit when allowed in the believer's life.

Everything here depends upon the assent of the will. Temptations to these sins do not grieve the Spirit, nor are temptations sins, but the moment the will assents to the practice or presence of these "and such like," the holy and sensitive Spirit is grieved. The *effect* of such assent of the will to "the law of sin which is in our members" is to refuse the rule of the Spirit in some part of our natures; to diminish the sphere of the Spirit's sway over us. Our complex nature is like an empire of many provinces. We are spirit, soul, and body. We may be willing that the Spirit shall control our ugly tempers, and yet indulge ourselves in settled bitterness. We may be willing that the Spirit shall rule our passions, and yet reserve what we are pleased to call the freedom of the intellect.

Before conversion this empire (though we were all unconscious of it) was ruled by Satan (I Corinthians 12:2; Ephesians 2:2) through self as viceroy. Now Christ is enthroned through the Spirit. But the dethroned ruler seeks ever the recovery of his dominion in whole, or in part; and the assent of the human will to any manifestation of the natural heart (Mark 8:20-23) is the re-enthronement of self and, in so far as self is allowed to act, the dethronement of Christ's vicegerent, the Spirit. It is not that He abandons us. Thank God we are "sealed unto the day of redemption," and "grieving away" the Spirit is an unbiblical notion, but a grieved Spirit is not an all-filling Spirit. The immediate consequence of the restriction of the sphere of the Spirit's authority is loss of blessing and victory in the inner life, and loss of power in the outer life—the life of service. The *remedy* for this loss, the filling of the Spirit, will be pointed out farther on.

(2) The *second* negative condition is stated in I Thessalonians 5:19, "Quench not the Spirit." The word (correctly rendered "quench") is used primarily of putting out fire; and in a secondary sense of resisting any vigorous effort. To quench the Spirit, therefore, is to resist His fiery energy, His consuming and purifying work. We are baptized with the Holy Ghost and with fire. He is the "Spirit of burning," and so of purification. He is also the Spirit of power. Through Him God lays hold upon us as instruments in a world-embracing purpose. To quench the Spirit therefore (let it be repeated) is to resist this twofold work of *purification* and of *use*. To reserve any dross of the natural man from the consuming action of this holy flame is, in so

far, to quench Him. Similarly, any resistance to His use of us, however slight, or from whatever cause, is to quench Him. The Spirit will not enforce obedience. His power is resistless, but waits the assent of our wills.

We quench the Spirit, therefore, when we oppose His will. We quench the Spirit, therefore, when we refuse to speak for Christ when consciously moved to do so by Him. It may seem a very small thing to us, but we are not qualified to judge concerning small and great in the estimation of God. In His work immense results often follow seemingly unimportant actions.

We quench the Spirit when we refuse His call to definite service.

We quench the Spirit when we refuse His absolute sovereignty over our service as to *what* (I Corinthians 12:8-11), *where* (Acts 8:2-4; 16:6, 7), and *how* (Acts 8:29) we shall serve Christ. So long as servants of

Christ are influenced in the place, kind, or method of their service by considerations of agreeableness, worldly advantage, salary and like motives, they may not hope to know His fullness.

We quench the Spirit when we consent to such arrangements in church life or organization as give no liberty for the ministry of the various gifts of the Spirit, thus imposing silence or inactivity on others.

The *effect* of quenching the Spirit is precisely the same with grieving Him—the sphere of His authority is diminished; we are no longer "filled," because we have excluded Him from some part of our being. An illustration of this was given in the last chapter in the case of the disciples who, filled on the day of Pentecost, needed to be and were filled again on a subsequent occasion.

The negative conditions of the filling with the Holy Spirit are, therefore, that we cease grieving Him by refusing the assent of the will to any unholiness; and that we cease quenching Him by opposing the resistance of the will to His sanctifying work *within* us, and His energizing work *upon* us.

It is not, let it again be insisted, that we are to make *ourselves* clean of sin, or to perfect ourselves in obedience. Neither of these acts is possible to us. In respect of both we are helpless. What we may do, is to put our wills over on the Spirit's side of these controversies. The representation is often made that if we can but will to be holy and obedient the victory is won. But, in the seventh chapter of Romans, Paul makes the tremendous and crushing discovery that willing and doing are by no means the same things. "For to will is present with me, but how to perform that which is good I find not" (Romans 7:18). Nor does he ever find it except in the mighty "law of the Spirit" (Romans 8:2).

We come now to—

2. *The positive conditions of the filling with the Holy Spirit.*

These are reducible to three. The *first*, variously stated in Scripture, as consecration, presenting the body a living sacrifice, taking up the cross, etc., is summed up finally in one word "yield." That is, yieldedness. "Neither yield ye your members as instruments of unrighteousness unto sin: but yield yourselves unto God, as those that are alive from the dead, and your members as instruments of righteousness unto God" (Romans 6:13).

The word here used for "yield," in its various forms in the original Greek, stands for the most absolute surrender to the control of another. In a slightly different form it is used by our Lord in Matthew 26:53, "Thinkest thou that I cannot now pray to my Father, and he shall presently *give me* [literally, 'yield'] more than twelve legions of angels?" Are we at liberty to suppose that those legions would think of obedience to Jesus in any but the most absolute sense? The word is used, also, of the presentation of sacrifices. These, needless to say, were wholly given to God. A sacrificer under the dispensation of law never dreamed of reasserting authority over a creature once brought to the priest. Indeed, his final act of authority was to slay his offering in the presence of the priest (Leviticus 4:33, etc.). The very thought of yieldedness, first of all, to death is enforced again and again in the Epistles (Romans 6:3, 6; 7:4; etc.). The very essence of true yieldedness is to consent that this judicial reckoning of God that we were crucified with Christ shall, *by the Spirit* (Romans 8:13), be made real in our experience (Galatians 5:24; II Corinthians 1:9; etc.). Let it be repeated that co-crucifixion with Christ is not a self-work—Christ did not crucify Himself—but as He "*through the Eternal Spirit* offered Himself" (Hebrews 9:14), so we "through the Spirit mortify ('make dead') the deeds of the body."

And this yieldedness is, be it observed, twofold—"yourselves," "your members." The first relates to the inner life—the sphere of soul and spirit as dominated by the flesh; the second to the outer life—the sphere of service. The first includes the yielding up to the Spirit of all things which defile us and therefore grieve Him. "Let all bitterness, and wrath, and anger, and clamor, and evil speaking *be put away from you*, with all malice." This is a very different thing from endeavoring ourselves to put these away. That we could never do; but the Holy Spirit can, and our yieldedness includes assent to this purifying work.

The yielding of our "members" as instruments is abandoning to Christ through the Spirit all control over our service as to *place, time,* or *quality.* Its formula is "anything, any time, anywhere." In Romans 12:1, this yieldedness is presented under the sacrificial form. Observe that the exhortation is not to sacrifice our bodies, but to *present* them (to our Priest) *for* sacrifice. The point for emphasis is the *utterness* of the abandonment of our bodies to Him. Under the old dispensation, as we have seen, the offerer had no secret purpose of reclaiming the offering. In the same way, to "yield" in the sense required, is sincerely, and honestly, and without any known secret reservation, to give self and our members over to the sway of Christ through the Spirit. Let now all possible emphasis be put upon the remaining truth about this yielding, *that it is a definite act.* Millions are never filled with the Holy Spirit, because they never definitely yield themselves and their members to God. Even among earnest Christians this lack of definiteness is proved by the practice of continually repeated consecrations (so-called). If we really have presented our bodies as living sacrifices, we clearly have nothing left to present. It is done.

The *second* positive condition of the filling is *faith*.

By faith is meant not our general trust in Christ as our Saviour, but trust in Him as the alone bestower of the Spirit. Let go all confusing *past* conditions, and remember that *now* and for *Christians* He, "being by the right hand of God exalted, and having received of the Father the promise of the Holy Ghost" (or "promised Holy Ghost"), is now in the precise position anticipated by Him when He uttered the words of John 7:37-39: "In the last day, that great day of the feast, Jesus stood and cried, saying, If any man thirst, let him come unto me and drink . . . but this spake he of the Spirit."

He has taken up the office of which

John the Baptist testified: "I indeed baptize you with water; but one mightier than I cometh, the latchet of whose shoes I am not worthy to unloose: he shall baptize you with the Holy Ghost and with fire" (Luke 3:16).

Just as He, during His earthly ministry, pointed to the Father as willing to give the Holy Spirit to those who should ask Him, so now the Holy Spirit points to the ascended and glorified Christ as the bestower of the Spirit (Acts 2:33).

Faith, then, is called upon here for a twofold exercise—to believe that the risen and glorified Christ is able and willing to bestow the fullness of the Spirit, and then to "drink" (John 7:37); that is, by a definite act of appropriation, to *receive* the Spirit. It is all of faith. One who has yielded self, and all known sin, and the body, unreservedly to the authority of Christ through the Spirit, is on taking ground. Heeding Christ's invitation, "If any man thirst let him come unto me and drink," he comes to Christ for this definite filling with the Spirit, and having come, he "drinks." It is precisely the same exercise of faith by which in the beginning of his Christian life he "received" Christ (John 1:12).

Just here multitudes who really thirst, who have honestly yielded the whole being to Christ, fail. Having come so near, they do not "drink." Waiting for some evidence of the senses they continue, perhaps for years, praying and longing for the fullness of the Spirit, but never "receive" Him. Perhaps, at last, they inwardly blame God. In the spirit of the elder son in the parable, they say, "Thou never gavest me a kid." The answer always is, "Son, all that I have is thine."

The *third* condition is *prayer*.

And this, be it remembered, is not asking

the Father for the Spirit. Jesus "being by the right hand of God exalted," has "received of the Father the promise of the Holy Ghost." Neither is it asking for the Holy Spirit in unbelief of the repeated and emphatic declarations that the believer now has the Spirit; nor, strictly speaking, is it asking for the fullness of the Spirit. In the wonderful prayer recorded in Acts 4:24-30 the disciples do not mention the Spirit. They pray about the fear they are in because of the Jewish religious authorities, and of "Herod and Pontius Pilate, with the Gentiles."

"Lord, behold their threatenings; and grant unto thy servants, that with all boldness they may speak thy word, by stretching forth thy hand to heal; and that signs and wonders may be done in the name of thy holy child Jesus."

Think of the directness, humility, and preoccupation with Christ, of that noble prayer, in contrast with the preoccupation with self, the subjectivity of so much latter-day praying about the Spirit. And, chiefly, note this: they prayed about the thing which had got wrong—"behold their threatenings." Fear was quenching the Spirit. So our prayers are to cover the ground of the most scrupulous and searching confession of failure, and of solicitude concerning the interests of Jesus, committed to our hands. To most, also, if not to all, prayer would be the most natural attitude of soul in definitely *receiving* the Spirit. How instinctively the expression would be: "Lord, I do receive; I am now receiving from Thee the fullness of the Spirit. I do believe Thou hast received of the Father the promise of the Holy Ghost, and Thou hast said, 'If any man thirst, let him come unto me and drink'; and so I drink."

One word of warning. The filling with the Spirit is both an *act* and a *process*; both an *event* and a *life*. There is a beginning of the state of fullness, but the continuance of that state depends upon the quiet, restful maintenance of the conditions. The believer who will know the blessedness of the Spirit-filled life must begin by definite acts of yieldedness, appropriating faith, and prayer; but he must also maintain as the habit of life, yieldedness, appropriating faith, and prayer. Confess instantly anything that grieves or quenches the Spirit—that maintains yieldedness. Be always "drinking" the Spirit. "He that *drinketh* of the water that I shall give him shall never thirst" (John 4:14). Keep the whole being in a receptive attitude toward the bestowing Christ. Do not try to think of the Spirit; think of Christ as the bestower of the Spirit. The holy and ever blessed and adorable Spirit would be well content to be quite out of our consciousness if only that consciousness were filled with Christ. Live the life of prayer. Use prayer to hide everything in the heart of God. Bathe the whole life and service in prayer. Then the life that begins with the filling will go on in the fullness.

A fruitful Christian is the result of a perpetual drinking at the fountain of "living waters." "I shall be anointed with fresh oil" (Psalm 92:10) should be the desire and the confident faith of every yielded servant of God as he goes forward to each new service.

The
Filling with
the Holy Spirit
Is Indispensable

5

The Filling with the Holy Spirit Is Indispensable

Much of the speaking about the filling with the Holy Spirit implies that such filling is desirable, indeed, but not indispensable. It is treated as one of the spiritual luxuries of the Christian life. A minister said to the writer, "I am going to look into that subject one of these days." He seemed utterly oblivious of the sorrowful fact that so long as he was not filled with the Spirit, no act of his service could be with power; and that because of that lack, his very sermon might work injury to his hearers, for nothing so surely causes atrophy of conscience and heart as *truth* divorced from *power* (II Timothy 3:5).

1. *No Christian should be willing to perform the slightest act in the service of Christ until he is definitely filled with the Holy Ghost.*

"And ye are witnesses of these things. And behold, I send the promise of my Father upon you, but tarry ye in the city of Jerusalem until ye be endued with power from on high" (Luke 24:48, 49). "But ye shall receive power after that the Holy Ghost is come upon you, and ye shall be witnesses unto me, both in Jerusalem and in all Judaea, and in Samaria, and unto the uttermost part of the earth" (Acts 1:8).

How wonderfully all this was fulfilled all readers of the second chapter of Acts know. After that the Holy Ghost was come upon them they *did* "receive power," for "they were all *filled* with the Holy Ghost, and began to speak with other tongues as the Spirit gave them utterance."

If, then, the very apostles of Jesus Christ, the chosen men who had been with Him and had been moulded by the tremendous impact of His personality; who were first-hand witnesses of His mighty miracles, and of His resurrection; whose memories were stored with His wonderful words, and who had received the indwelling Spirit by His direct outbreathing—if *those* men must tarry until they were filled with the Spirit before beginning even the least service, is it not a dangerous and disobedient self-confidence for one of us to begin a service without the filling?

Nor, Biblically, is the filling with the Holy Spirit indispensable only to ministers of the Word. The filling is indispensable for *any* service.

"And in those days, when the number of

the disciples was multiplied, there arose a murmuring of the Grecians against the Hebrews, because their widows were neglected in the daily ministration. Then the twelve called the multitude of the disciples unto them, and said: "It is not reason that we should leave the word of God and serve tables. Wherefore, brethren, look ye out among you seven men of honest report, *full of the Holy Ghost* and of wisdom, whom we may appoint over this business" (Acts 6:1-3).

Just as in the Jewish dispensation, Bezaleel was "filled with the Spirit of God" to "work in gold, and in silver, and in brass," because God would teach us that *all* acceptable ministry, even though mechanical, was acceptable only when rendered by a Spirit-prepared servant; so in the church age, He would commit even the temporalities of the church only to men qualified in the same way. In other words, it is the method of God's appointment. How great would be the peace and prosperity of the Church of God if all ministers and office-bearers were filled with the Spirit!

The writer believes that all this is most solemn. What is the attempted service of an unfilled Christian but an insolent attempt to override the order of God? It is no uncharity to say that the inevitable result of such service is the attempt to substitute fleshly expedients for the lacking spiritual power.

——Look over the church notices of any city newspaper, and see how feverish and frantic are the attempts to substitute "attractions" for power. It is the sin of Nadab and Abihu; and, as their sin was punished by physical death, so in modern religious life the anti-typical sin of the substition of strange fire for Spirit fire is punished by awful spiritual deadness.

2. *No Christian can possibly live a right*

Christian life who is not filled with the Holy Spirit.

All of the varied offices of the Spirit as indwelling the believer—offices bearing upon the believer's inner life—depend for their vigorous ministry upon the filling with the Spirit. One may have the Spirit, and yet live a carnal, joyless life. The case of the Corinthian church demonstrates this (1 Corinthians 1:2-9, 11-13; 3:1-4; 5:1, 2; 6:6). It is when the Christian is filled with the Spirit that all the marvellous results of His indwelling are realized.

When it is remembered that it is the Spirit who gives victory over sin (Romans 8:2; Galatians 5:16, 17); actualizes to the believer his position in Christ (Galatians 3:26; 4:6); produces the fragrant fruits of "love, joy, peace, long-suffering, gentleness, goodness, faith, meekness, and temperance" (Galatians 5:22, 23); imparts spiritual vigor, strengthening him "with might in the inner man" (Ephesians 3:16); indites his prayers (Romans 8:26; Ephesians 6:18; comforts him (John 14:16, 17); guides him, sanctifies him and makes of him a "true" worshipper, it should be evident that, since every believer *may* be filled with the Holy Spirit, he is most flagrantly guilty before God if he is not so filled.

In other words, it is not open to the believer without serious guilt to be living in known sin, serving self, and barren of the "much fruit" which alone glorifies the Father (John 15:8). God, in grace, has by the Spirit made possible to every believer a saintly life and a powerful service. No Christian minister should be content without the conversion of sinners and the up-building of saints, for both are within His power. True, there may be churches so deliberately set in worldliness and unspirituality that they reject the ministry of the Spirit, however tenderly and wisely offered. Very well, let a Spirit-filled minister turn from such a church, even though weeping over it as Christ wept over Jerusalem, and God will assuredly give him a hearing elsewhere. But let him be sure first that he *has* offered a Spirit-filled ministry. And (let it be repeated) no believer, whether layman or minister, should be content one hour without the ineffable blessedness of a Spirit-filled life.

One final, but (in the light of much which is said and written) necessary word as to the ground of the Christian's assurance of the filling. Much is said, most harmfully as the writer believes, concerning consciousness. The harm done by that word lies in identifying it with *feeling*. It seems to be supposed that the Christian who definitely and continuously yields himself and his members, and who has really been filled with the Spirit, will know it by *feeling* holy, or powerful. That, in a word, he will be conscious of the Spirit. Nothing can be more misleading. Spirit-filled men are deeply conscious of what Matthew Henry calls "manifold defects and shortcomings in holy duties." But they are conscious, too, of the nearness, the beauty, the abounding love, the holiness and tenderness of Christ, and of the power of His blood to perfectly cleanse from all sin. New discoveries of sin but send them again and again to that cleansing stream. Their consciousness, then, is Christ-consciousness, not Spirit-consciousness. Doubtless there is a holy exercise of the emotions. "The fruit of the Spirit is . . . joy." There is a "righteousness and peace and joy in the Holy Ghost." But there are also seasons of "weakness and fear and much trembling," and these often accompany the "demonstrations of the Spirit and of power" (I Corinthians 2:3, 4).

Cast far away, then, as a snare to the soul, the watchfulness of subjective frames and feelings and stand by faith. Just as we believe that Christ has given us eternal life because He said, "Verily, verily, I say unto you he that believeth on me hath eternal life" (John 6:47), so we believe that He who bids the thirsty to "come unto Him and drink," *does* give the rivers of blessing and power to those who drink. And to all who thus stand by faith He, in due season, grants to see the rivers, and to know the blessed cleansing and refreshing of the up-springing fountain.